The Making of Irish Linen

Historic photographs of an Ulster industry

Peter Collins

FRIAR'S BUSH PRESS

INTRODUCTION

This photographic collection encapsulates the history of the Irish linen industry for which Ulster was so justifiably famous throughout the world. Today linen has no longer the supreme economic and social significance that it had for so many generations, but it is still an important local employer. The making of linen is age old, being one of the first three products, along with bread and wine, mentioned in the Old Testament. The earliest written record of linen in Ireland is in 13th century monastic sources in Armagh, Bangor and Newtownards, though it is likely to have been in production long before then. However, it did not become really important in Ireland until the 17th century. This was due to the efforts of Wentworth, later the Earl of Strafford, then Lord Deputy who gave preferential treatment to the Irish linen industry at a time when the Irish wool trade was severely restricted by prohibitive government tariffs on exports into England. This was to protect the English wool industry against Irish competition. Wentworth encouraged the introduction of new methods and brought better seed from the continent in order to encourage the Irish linen industry to develop as a trade-off for the destruction of the wool industry.

The government encouraged the coming to the north of Ireland of some 500 families of Huguenots, French protestants. Fleeing persecution, by Louis XIV, at the end of the seventeenth century, they brought with them skills which were to take root in Ulster and out of which grew a widespread cottage industry. A leading Huguenot, Louis Crommelin, was given the grandiose title, 'Overseer of the Royal Linen Manufacture' and had a great influence over the development of the industry from the base which these immigrants had established in Lisburn and the Lagan valley. It was not only immigrants who assisted the development of the industry. Landlords, especially Lord Conway, Lord Hillsborough and the Brownlows in Lurgan as well as the London livery companies in the Coleraine area, set in train important development work. Samuel Waring of Waringstown, in the late 17th century, imported a colony of Flemish weavers who brought with them improved methods entirely new to Ireland. In addition, a linen board was established in 1711 to oversee the development of the industry. The board functioned for over a century, during which time the industry moved from cottage to factory production. This came about, in the early nineteenth century, due to the proliferation of inventions in the textile industry in Britain and America. The application of these spread rapidly, due to the effective juxtaposition of surplus capital and entrepreneurial initiative that characterised the period of the industrial revolution in Ulster.

Cotton, the principal textile in the British Isles, was supplanted in Ulster by linen, early in the last century, as a result of inventions which allowed wet spinning of fine linen yarns and powerloom weaving. A catalyst to the introduction of these new processes was the accidental burning down of the Mulholland Brothers cotton weaving factory in Belfast in the 1820s. In rebuilding, they decided to make the switch to linen and such was their success that many other manufacturers followed suit. This led to the growth of a huge number of linen spinning mills in and around Belfast. The temporary unavailability of cotton, during the American civil war, led to a big demand for linen in the 1850s and 1860s, which was to persist. The number of mills in Belfast grew from one in 1831 to 32 in 1861. This was mirrored in other towns such as Lisburn, Banbridge and Lurgan, and mill villages such as Waringstown, Bessbrook and Sion Mills.

While the Lagan valley became the main area of linen production, purpose built mill villages were important in other areas. The earliest of these was Barbour's Plantation built near Lisburn in 1784. Others included F.W. Hayes' mill and village at Seapatrick near Banbridge, Co. Down; Upperlands, Co. Derry (William Clark & Sons); Mossley, Co. Antrim (Edmund Grimshaw); Muckamore, Co. Antrim (William Chaine); Shrigley, near Killyleagh, Co. Down (John Martin); Drumaness, Co.Down (Charles James Hurst); Milford, Co. Armagh (McCrum, Watson & Mercer Ltd); and Edenderry, Co. Antrim (John Shaw Brown). Dunbarton at Gilford was built in the 1820s by Dunbar McMaster and Company. Donaghcloney, Co. Down, was the home of William Liddell & Co. In all of these, with the exception of Gilford, there had been some spinning or weaving in existence. They were little self-contained industrial communities, in many respects resembling the American company town. The employers planned the villages with well-designed housing, schools, libraries, community centres and plenty of recreational activities, especially cricket. This contrasted favourably with the lot of many industrial workers in the larger urban centres.

Most important were Sion Mills, Co.Tyrone, built by Herdmans in 1835 and Bessbrook, Co. Armagh established in the 1840s by the Quaker Richardson family. In the case of Bessbrook, the Richardsons were very protective of the moral welfare of the inhabitants ensuring the absence of the three p's, police barracks, public houses and pawnshops. In addition they had a contributory health service for workers long before the Welfare State and even a savings scheme, yielding interest of 5%. Indeed Bessbrook became the model for the village of Bournville built in the 1890s by the Quaker chocolate manufacturers, the Cadbury family. In both Sion Mills and Bessbrook a real feeling of community spirit was engendered in the workers due to their environment, which made them the envy of their counterparts elsewhere in the linen industry. Herdman's is still in business but the Bessbrook Spinning Company closed down in 1972, although the village is still well worth visiting. All the workers got redundancy payments and were able to buy their houses at very low cost. With the decline in importance of linen in the years since the war and the increased mobility of the population, the mill villages have changed both in their physical composition and their sense of community.

Expansion was fuelled by a good supply of swift flowing water and Scottish coal that could be brought more cheaply by sea to Belfast than overland to most of the industrial centres of Britain. The Irish linen manufacturers kept their product to the forefront, in competition with the less expensive cotton, by stressing its superiority in household and clothing use, and by an aggressive marketing policy in the expanding markets of the empire and north and south America. This was backed up by considerable investment in research and development which was characteristic of the progressive business attitude of the linen industrialists. However in some sectors of the industry, the conditions and low earnings of the workers often provided a bleak contrast to this air of general progress.

For example, much of the finishing was done by women in their own homes at very low piece rates. The Government Linen Inquiry of 1912, looked at 531 cases out of the reported 4,000 outworkers in the Belfast area. Of these 497 were paid less than 3d an hour, 422 less than 2d and 269 earned 1d or less per hour at a time when a loaf of bread was about 6d and rent for such workers about five shillings a week.

In 1913 a list of the largest firms in the Irish linen industry, published in a trade directory by John Warral Ltd of Oldham, showed the York Street Flax Spinning Co.(Ltd), the company founded by the Mulhollands, as the largest spinning and weaving concern with 63,000 spindles and a thousand looms. J.& T.M.Greeves (Ltd) was the largest spinning company with 70,000 spindles. Milfort Weavers with factories in Belfast and Dunmurry were the largest weaving concerns in Ulster with 1,000 looms. The industry generally remained prosperous, up to the First World War. As a result of that war, production reached a new peak with the need for materials for uniforms and coverings for aircraft wings and fuselages. Indeed Field Marshal Lord French declared in 1919 that, *'The war was won on Ulster wings'*.

However, after the war, in common with cotton, linen manufacture entered a slow process of decline. In 1920 there were about fifty spinning companies in Ulster of which seventeen were in Belfast. At the same time there were some 35,000 power looms in about a hundred weaving factories. By the depressed nineteen-thirties, production was less than forty per cent of the pre-war figure. In 1939 only 59,000 were employed out of a total registered workforce of 72,000. This decline was arrested temporarily by the second world conflict. Linen again contributed in many ways to the war effort. By 1945 the number in work had declined to 40,000, although this had recovered to about 55,000 by 1950. The 1950s saw linen and cotton, in the United Kingdom, marginalised by the explosion of man-made fibres, cheap cotton imports from the Far East and paper products. Indeed, the growth of man-made fibre production in Ulster itself contributed to the demise of linen. By the 1970s the labour force had gone down by about half from the 1950 figure. Of late there has been somewhat of a renaissance in linen with burgeoning demand from the luxury end of the market, particularly in high fashion.

GROWING AND HARVESTING FLAX

SOWING THE FLAX, TOOME, CO. ANTRIM, *c.* 1915.

The process of growing, harvesting and turning flax into linen was long and complex. First, the flax seed was either grown locally or imported from places as far apart as Russia, Belgium and the United States. Imported seed was usually preferred although the additional expense limited its use to the better-off grower. Flax was sown in the spring and by mid-summer it had beautiful pale blue flowers.

The crop was ready for harvesting about a hundred days after sowing. It was carefully watched as it was important to harvest it only when the fibre was at its best. The sign that the seed was ripe was when the colour changed from green to pale brown, usually in early September or late August in a good year. (Green Coll.)

PULLING FLAX, DROMARA, CO. DOWN, 1920.

Unlike other plants flax was not cut but pulled, roots and all. This was in order that no part of the stem was wasted and to ensure that the fibres were as long as possible. It was extremely hard on those involved 'pulling lint', as it was known colloquially, leaving the labourer with an aching back and bloodied hands. (Welch Coll.)

RIPPLING FLAX, FORTWILLIAM GOLF CLUB, BELFAST, FIRST WORLD WAR.

Where seed was required, it was removed by a process known as rippling, whereby the flax was pulled through iron teeth on a wooden block, thus separating the seed from the stem. In wartime, seed was at a premium due to the suspension of imports from Russia, France and Belgium. As well as golf clubs, unused fields in the city were put under cultivation; for example, waste ground behind Mackie's Foundry on the Springfield Road, Belfast was used for flax for the duration. (Hogg Coll.)

RETTING, BALLYNAHINCH, CO. DOWN, *c.* 1910.

After pulling, the beets were put into ponds or dams of still water, known as the 'lint-hole', for the process called retting. This rotted and softened the stems and broke down the pectin, a substance which held together the flax fibre, the woody core and the outer cover. The beets were kept in the lint-hole for some eight to fourteen days and the time for removal was signalled by the heightening of a noxious smell caused by the fermentation process. Removal was also extremely hard work with the labourers standing up to their waists in cold stinking water to lift out the heavy sodden beets. (Welch Coll.)

GAITING OR BUNDLING, DROMARA, CO. DOWN, *c.* 1930.

The flax was drained for a few hours in stooks on the banks of the 'lint-hole'. It was then 'grassed', that is laid out in 'spread fields' for six to twelve days to allow the sun and wind to dry it and to help the fibres separate from the other parts of the plant. Finally it was sent in bundles to the scutch mill. (*Belfast Telegraph*)

PULLING FLAX THROUGH A BREAKER, TOOME, CO. ANTRIM, *c*.1915.
In the early days, the preparation of yarn was done by hand or powered by water wheel in three processes; breaking, scutching and hackling. Later these were mechanised. Breaking, on grooved rollers, broke up the outer skin and the wooden core of the plant. (Green Coll.)

OLD SCUTCH MILL EXTERIOR, BRYANSFORD, CO. DOWN, *c.* 1910.
Flax was scutched between flat wooden blades which removed the
skin and core, leaving only the fibres. The scutched fibre went on to
market where, in more modern times, it was purchased at a standard
price set by the cooperative purchasing agency representing all the
spinning companies. (Welch Coll.)

ROUGHING, BRAIDWATER MILL, CO. ANTRIM, *c.*1935.
Roughing was the preliminary combing of the fibre to straighten it
out to prepare for spinning. The rougher picks a handful of fibres, flicks it to open like a fan and draws it over a series of pins.
(*Belfast Telegraph*)

CARDING AND COMBING DEPARTMENT, LINDSAY, THOMPSON AND CO. LTD, MULHOUSE WORKS, GROSVENOR ROAD, BELFAST, 1938.

Carding and combing was part of the overall process of roughing in which the impurities known as 'neps' were removed by combing on machines which also squared the ends of the fibre to allow it to be gripped in the hackling. The conditions for workers in this end of the spinning mill were particularly bad because of the inhalation of dust, known to the workers as 'pouce'. Disorders of the chest and lungs were common and the life expectancy of these workers was low.

The certifying officer for the Belfast factory district reported in graphic terms the effects on such workers: '*When about thirty years, their appearance begins to alter, the face gets an anxious look, shoulders begin to get rounded – in fact they become prematurely aged and the greater number die before forty-five years of age.*' (C.D. Purdon, *Sanitary state of the Belfast factory district*, 1877, p12. (Belfast Exposed)

MACHINE HACKLING, HAYE'S MILL, SEAPATRICK, NEAR BANBRIDGE, CO. DOWN, *c.*1910.
After roughing, the next stage of this process was hackling, a more scientific combing in which the fibres were untangled, removing any remaining useless matter. The separate lengths of fibre were combed into one continuous ribbon known as the 'sliver'. This was done on a 'spreader', attached to the hackling machine. It then emerged like the human hair which is often flatteringly described as 'flaxen'. It was now ready for spinning. (Welch Coll.)

DRAWING AT THOMAS SINTON & CO. LTD, TANDRAGEE, CO. ARMAGH, IN THE EARLY 1960s.
In this the 'sliver', a ribbon of even weight, was regularised in width by 'drawing' on a series of rollers on drawing frames. On the left is Mrs Cookson and on the right Mrs McClean. Sinton's is one of the longest surviving linen firms. It has been in continuous existence since the 1880s and is still run by the same family. (Thos Sinton & Co. Ltd)

HAND SCUTCHING, TOOME, CO. ANTRIM, *c.* 1915.
Linen production was an important cottage industry which supplemented the income from farming in many parts of Ulster up to the late nineteenth century. It survived in some areas as late as the 1920s. (Green Coll.)

HACKLING FLAX BY HAND, TOOME, CO. ANTRIM, c. 1915.
When W.A. Green, the photographer, was visiting a friend in Toome, he became aware of a proliferation of linen skills in the area. He was so interested that he stayed a fortnight while the friend drove him about. He recorded this in a paper given in 1921 to the Belfast Natural History and Philosophical Society, entitled 'Photography as an Aid to Nature Study': '*I got pictures of several of the the old methods used in the country in the manipulation of flax; hand scutching, breaking, cloving, hand hackling etc. Curiously enough most of the people engaged in these primitive operations are since dead, and as they appear to be the last to use them, I think they are now obsolete*'. (Green Coll.)

MRS ANNIE COLLINS, THE LAST LOOM HARNESS MAKER, WARINGSTOWN, CO. DOWN, MARCH 27, 1914.

The number of handloom weavers had greatly declined by the time of this photograph. Mrs Collins is getting the 'harness', that is the yarn and equipment, ready for the loom. It was obviously brought out of the house for a posed picture. On the left is the 'swift' on which the hanks of yarn are spread. They are then reeled onto the warping frame for the loom. In the centre is the spinning wheel, with the smaller wheel behind used for winding weft or cross-thread yarn for the pirns, which are set in the shuttle. Further right is the clock or 'click' reel, used for measuring off lengths of yarn. Its circumference was 2.25 yards, so 40 turns added up to 100 yards. On the far right is the warping frame on which the longitudinal warp yarn was wound onto spools. (*Belfast Telegraph*)

14

HANDLOOM WEAVER, MOIRA, CO. DOWN, *c.* 1910.
The introduction of the hand loom and the skills brought by
Huguenots enabled a significant domestic linen weaving industry to
exist in Ulster from the early eighteenth century. This basis of the
cottage linen industry was largely supplanted by power looms in the
late nineteenth century. However, pockets survived in some areas for
various local reasons though the skill usually died with the individual
weaver. Hand loom weaving is now kept alive only in a museum
setting as at the Ulster Folk and Transport Museum at Cultra,
Co. Down, or in craft workshops. (Green Coll.)

WOMAN DOING DRAWN THREAD WORK, MOIRA, CO. DOWN, *c.* 1910.

Intricate embroidery was a feature of the linen industry, employing thousands of women outworkers in the rural cottages and the poorer terraces of Belfast and Derry and the linen towns and villages of Ulster. The strength of the linen weave made it particularly amenable to embroidery and holes could be made in it, with sharp piercers, around which the fancy stitching was done without damaging the cloth. Indeed the embroidering of Irish linen was also often done abroad in places as far apart as Madeira, the Canary Islands, China and Japan, with designs more appropriate to those countries. (Green Coll.)

WIDOW GREER 'FLOWERING', WREN'S NEST, BRYANSFORD, CO. DOWN, *c.* 1910.

Flowering or sprigging were terms to denote the embroidered decoration of cloth. Bryansford, like many similar villages throughout Ulster, had a long established tradition of embroidery. Indeed Bassett's guide and directory for Co. Down in 1886 lists an embroidery school in Bryansford, where the mistress was Miss Bella Bailie. (Welch Coll.)

SPINNING

ISLAND SPINNING MILL, LISBURN, CO. ANTRIM, *c.*1950.
The wet spinning process, invented by James Kay of Preston in 1825, involved a six hour soaking of the linen yarn in cold water which prevented it from snapping, thus allowing mechanised spinning. Wet spinning was introduced in the north of Ireland two years later, the first successful commercial venture being that of Murland's of Annsborough near Castlewellan, County Down. The spinning mill was usually four stories high. Roughing, hackling and other preparation was done on the first floor. Spinning rooms occupied the next two floors, while the lighter reeling and winding machinery was installed on the top storey. The yarn was sent from there down a chute to the drying area set aside from the main building, usually over the boiler room. An average mill employed about 750 people mostly women, though the managers, overseers, and maintenance staff were all men. (Irish Linen Centre, Lisburn Museum)

DOFFERS IN THE 1940s, BELFAST.

It was the doffer's job to see that the spinning frames were stopped at the appropriate time. The filled bobbins were removed, thrown into boxes and empty bobbins were put on to the spindles. The spinning frame was set ready for motion again. The full bobbins were then taken to the reeling room. Incidentally, the machinery bears the trademark of James Reynolds &Co. Ltd, Linfield Road, Belfast. An offshoot of the linen industry was the proliferation of textile engineering and foundry firms that grew up to supply the machinery. This resulted in a freestanding industry that exported machinery worldwide. (*Belfast Telegraph*)

DOFFERS, BLACKSTAFF FLAX SPINNING AND WEAVING CO. LTD, SPRINGFIELD ROAD, BELFAST.

This photograph taken in the 1920s, includes Mrs McKeown of Plevna Street, Lower Falls Road, third person in, second row from back. The bare feet were a consequence of having to stand in fetid water as part of the wet spinning process. Many doffers indeed wore no shoes to and from work even in winter and skinned and hacked skin was common. They are bedecked with the tools of the doffer; hackle pins for digging out broken ends from bobbins, scrapers and pickers used for removing pieces of rove that got wound round the roller. The doffing mistress, on the right, had a whistle. It was her job to decide when to stop the spinning frame for doffing. (Belfast Exposed)

DOFFERS AND 'HALF-TIMERS' IN THE FALLS AREA OF BELFAST IN THE 1920s.

'Half-timers' were children who worked in linen mills for half a day before attending school in the afternoon. The practice varied in different areas, with some attending school and working on alternate days. These children were often an indispensable factor in the economic survival of low-income families. The effect on their education can be gauged from the fact that of the 139 half-timers attending St Gall's National School between 1902 and 1905, only fifteen went on to standard five. The practice was dying out by the 1920s and the 1930 Northern Ireland Education Act made it illegal. (Belfast Exposed)

THE REELING ROOM, WILLIAM EWART & SON LTD, BELFAST, *c.* 1890.

William Quartus Ewart, the founder of the firm was Conservative MP for Belfast 1878–85 and North Belfast 1885–89. Ewart's with offices in Bedford Street, had mills and factories on the Crumlin Road and at Ligoniel. This photograph, taken in the early 1900s, shows reeling rooms where the yarn was wound on to large revolving frames. Reelers were regarded as the aristocrats among mill girls and the cleaner nature of their work allowed them to wear normal clothes with shoes and stockings. They did, however, wear a 'patch', a canvas apron to protect their skirt when they stopped the reel with their knee. The reelers were often on piecework and consequently depended on the spinners for a constant supply of adequately filled bobbins. If this was not forthcoming there would be friction between the two groups. (Lawrence Coll.)

BUNDLING YARN AT UNNAMED MILL, c. 1915.
A view of the mill area with the drive belts and yarn bundles. After reeling, the yarn was put into a heated drying loft or drying machine where it was not made bone dry but conditioned to an optimum moisture content for future processes. It was then made up in bundles of 60,000 yards for sale as 'grey' or unbleached yarn. (Green Coll.)

WILLIAM BARBOUR'S LINEN THREAD WORKS, DUNMURRY, CO. ANTRIM, *c.* 1920.

In 1784 the first thread works in Ireland was set up by John Barbour, a Scot from Paisley. The business he established is still carried on today at Hilden near Lisburn. Thread was sold throughout the world to many different customers in, for example, shoemaking and other leatherwork, medical, clothing and domestic use. In addition to Hilden, Dunmurry and Sprucefield, Barbour's had factories in Germany; New Jersey; and Pennsylvania. In the 1890s Barbours employed 1,200 in their Paterson, New Jersey plant and had opened another one in Allentown, Pennsylvania. Many linen firms had agents, branches and travellers in the United States. The United States was a huge market taking half of all exports of Irish linen in 1914. (Green Coll.)

COMMEMORATING TEN YEARS OF THE BARBOUR'S OTTENSEN FACTORY HAMBURG, *c*.1898.
There was a big market for Irish linen world wide, so firms set up factories, branches and agencies in Europe, north and south America and the empire. Germany was Britain's greatest trading competitor but also a major market despite the protectionist stance of its government. Clearly this was a consideration for Barbour's in starting production in Hamburg. (Irish Linen Centre, Lisburn Museum)

THE ROYAL DAMASK CO. LTD, ARDOYNE, BELFAST, *c.* 1890.
This company was founded in 1823, by Michael Andrews, who was the first Irish linen manufacturer to adapt damask handlooms to the Jacquard method. The original name of the company was the 'Royal Manufactory of Linen and Damask'. It was renowned for the very high standard of its damask. (Welch Coll.)

DURHAM STREET WEAVING FACTORY, BELFAST IN THE 1960s.
This is a weaving factory in the Lower Falls, Belfast, surrounded by linen workers' houses with the twin spires of St Peter's catholic cathedral in the background. It was known to its workers as 'the Pound' after a stream of that name which also became the name of the district. The photograph shows the close proximity of houses to the mills and factories which dominated local communities in Belfast. There was no escaping the noises and smells exuding from them, starting off with the early morning whistle or siren summoning the workers. (Linen Hall Library)

WINDING WEFT YARN, YORK STREET FACTORY, BELFAST, *c.* 1935.
The introduction in 1850 of the power loom enabled one worker to do the work of four hand-loom weavers. Immediately enterprising manufacturers set up power-loom weaving factories which soon matched the mechanisation of spinning. Like the spinning mill, the weaving factories were usually four stories high. The heavy machinery of the weaving shed was always on the flat. Above that was the weft winding. On the third storey, winding the warp was done and on the top, in the dressing shop, adhesive material was added to lay down loose fibres and strengthen the yarn. The first process in the weaving factory was in the winding room. (*Belfast Telegraph*)

OPERATING A WARPING MACHINE, THE ULSTER WEAVING COMPANY, BELFAST, *c.*1955.

In warping, the longitudinal yarn was wound onto spools. From these the threads were separated and arranged and fed to a warping beam or roller in such a way as to allow them to roll out lengthwise on to the loom. The warp yarns, which ran lengthwise in the fabric, were of considerable length to allow continuous weaving of a long web of cloth. The Ulster Weaving Works was situated in the Sandy Row area of Belfast. It was known to its workers, in its early days, as 'Tea Lane' from the houses on the lane leading up to it, where the half-doors were kept open and tea left on the hearth, ready for anyone who might drop in. The company is still in business. (*Belfast Telegraph*)

THE WINDING ROOM, McCRUM, WATSON & MERCER, MILFORD, CO. ARMAGH, 1910.

Milford was started as a spinning mill in 1808, by William McCrum, in the townland of Kennedies, about two miles south of Armagh city, but it soon changed to damask weaving. The making of linen ceased there in 1986. In this picture the workers are from left to right, Mary Bains, M. J. Delaney, Kate Fields and Agnes Quinn. In the background, we can just about make out Annie Wallace, James Gillen and Kate McFarland. (Allison Coll.)

A PLAIN POWER LOOM WEAVING SHOP, BROOKFIELD FACTORY, YORK STREET, BELFAST, *c.* 1900.

Before 1850, Ireland had only 58 power looms compared to over a thousand in England and two and a half thousand in Scotland weaving linen. This was because the low wages of handloom weavers in Ireland made the industry economically competitive without automation. Also power looms could only weave coarse linen. However, in the 1850s power looms were adapted to weave the fine linens that made up the bulk of Irish production. The increased demand for linen caused by the American civil war, led to a rush of power loom introduction and by the 1870s, there were some fifteen thousand in Ireland. In 1910 the figure had reached thirty five thousand. (Welch Coll.)

JACQUARD POWER LOOMS, EWART'S MILL, BELFAST, OCTOBER 1930.

This shows the punched pattern cards suspended over the weaving machines. The Jacquard innovation, developed in Lyons, France in 1804, consisted of a small frame, known as an 'engine', added to an existing loom. Because it was compact, it could be used in either the cottage or the factory. It was a major advance in weaving. The Jacquard process was harnessed to power looms in the 1870s and soon became a feature in the rise of factory damask weaving. (Hogg Coll.)

PUNCHING PATTERN CARDS FOR DOUBLE DAMASK WEAVING, WARINGSTOWN, CO. DOWN, *c.* 1910.

An essential prerequisite to the Jacquard weaving process was a series of punch cards onto which the pattern, already hand drawn by the designer, was transferred as a series of holes. It enabled a primitive form of automation in weaving. The weaver could put the cards through the 'engine' in sequence by means of foot treadles. This caused selected threads to be raised so the pattern indicated on the punch cards was woven into the cloth. The Jacquard process enabled a hand-loom weaver to work on damask at home on his own rather than as before with as many as sixteen helpers. (Green Coll.)

DOUBLE DAMASK POWER LOOM, WARINGSTOWN, CO.
DOWN, *c.* 1910.
Weaving on power looms was first introduced in the 1850s. In 1869
Henry Barcroft of Bessbrook Spinning Company introduced the
Bessbrook self-twilling machine, which enabled damasks to be woven
on power looms fitted with the Jacquard mechanism. Damasks woven
on such power looms were exhibited at the Philadelphia Centennial
Exhibition in 1876 and were such a success that liveried Irish damask
became the standard in luxury hotels, railways and ocean liners, the
world over. Nevertheless ultra-high quality hand woven damask
continued to be produced as gifts for visiting celebrities such as heads
of state. (Green Coll.)

DAMASK DESIGNERS, MILFORD FACTORY, ARMAGH, 1904.
Design was an important factor in the success of Irish linen
particularly in the production of damask. Many firms employed
designers and Belfast College of Technology had a school of textile
design which was the equal of any in the world. This picture shows
damask designs being produced for hotels and railways in the United
States and elsewhere. (Allison Coll.)

BLEACH GREEN, NEAR BELFAST, IN THE EARLY 1900s.
After weaving, the cloth known as brown linen was sent for bleaching. The linen was bleached either by exposure to the elements or by a chemical process. In the former case it was laid out for an extended period on a south facing slope. The bleach green became a feature of the Ulster landscape, the long lines of cloth contrasting with the emerald grass. (Lawrence Coll.)

BLEACHING HANDKERCHIEFS, THE GREEN, KIRKPATRICK BROTHERS, BALLYCLARE, CO. ANTRIM, 1934.

Herbie Watts, Ned Hollis and Johnny Millar working on the last field of handkerchiefs to be bleached at the Green. The greatest total output for one week at Kirkpatrick Bros. bleach and dye works was 110 tons, in 1918, when they employed over 500. (R.T. Grange)

KIRKPATRICK BROTHERS, MAIN OFFICE BLOCK, *c.* 1910.
This was one of the oldest bleach works in Ireland, having continuously operated on this site since the middle of the eighteenth century. It was a major source of employment in the east Antrim area. This office block was constructed by the British Bleachers Association which took over the company at the start of the century.

The saw-edge north-light roof on a two storey block presents an unusual spectacle. Kirkpatrick's closed in 1966, the present occupiers being Kirkpatrick-Linron (Ballyclare) Ltd, specialists in the combined use of flax and man-made fibres. (G. McKeown)

DIPPING LINEN IN THE BLEACHING PROCESS, c. 1915.
Grass bleaching was largely superseded by the use of chemicals, particularly chlorine, in bleach works. The cloth was then washed many times in huge machines till it was white. Sometimes a combination of 'grassing' and chemical bleaching was used. (Green Coll.)

'BLUEING', MUCKAMORE, CO. ANTRIM, *c.* 1905.

This was part of the finishing process conducted after bleaching. The pieces to be finished to a given length were sewn together, passed through a steam mangle and plaited. The cloth was dried over steam cylinders and then separated into individual pieces prior to beetling.

The other finishing processes included calendering and mangling, all designed to achieve various types of finish. Afterwards the cloth might have been sent for printing or dyeing. (Welch Coll.)

TENDING A BEETLING MACHINE, *c.* 1915.
An important process in finishing the cloth was beetling. In this the cloth was wrapped around large slowly revolving rollers while wooden blocks or beetles pounded it at up to four hundred blows a minute, hammering it to a fine glossy finish thus bringing out its natural lustre. This also tightened the weave to eliminate small gaps.

The harnessing of water power enabled the introduction of beetling engines to rural areas and by the middle of the eighteenth century they were commonplace, throughout the north of Ireland. The clatter of the hundreds of hammers was characterisic of the area. Beetlers stood a good chance of going deaf. (Green Coll.)

BLEACHING DEPARTMENT, KIRKPATRICK'S, BALLYCLARE, CO. ANTRIM, 1940.
Unlike the other areas of the industry, where women generally made up three-quarters of the workforce, bleaching had a much higher proportion of male employees. In this particular department men form the majority. (R.T. Grange)

FINISHED PRODUCTS

MAGHERA EMBROIDERY SCHOOL INTERIOR, CO. DERRY, 1913.
The linen industry also gave rise to many other skills and trades in Ulster. The cloth was involved in further finishing processes before it reached the consumer, including dyeing and embroidering such items as fine underclothes, shirts, and household linen. The embroidery school in Maghera was concerned with special training on Swiss machinery which turned out batches of thirteen dozen embroidered handkerchiefs. In the picture the embroidery of the master design is being done (at one sixth of its size) on the fabric, by using a pantograph. (Hogg Coll.)

LINEN HANDKERCHIEF MANUFACTURE, NELSON BELL & CO. BEDFORD STREET, BELFAST, IN THE 1920s.

There is a Cambrai Street in the Shankill linen manufacturing area, called after the French town from which cambric takes its name. This cloth, used in dresses and handkerchiefs, requires a very fine yarn. Irish linen handkerchiefs dominated the luxury end of the world market. In 1879 George Benson of Belfast designed a sewing machine for the hemstitching of handkerchiefs. This reduced costs which helped market-share worldwide and increased employment in the making-up trades. Finishing handkerchiefs and cuffs as well as embroidery was also done by outworkers. (PRONI)

STITCHERS IN THE SEWING ROOM, ALEXANDER BOOM & CO., BELFAST, IN THE 1920s.
Stitching was often done in factories which were no more than 'sweatshops'. This photograph, taken by Robert Lyttle of 44

Dublin Rd, Belfast, a professional photographer (1910–1931) was not concerned to highlight the negative side of this work. (PRONI)

LITTLE'S SHIRT FACTORY, SPENCER ROAD, DERRY, IN THE 1930s.
In the case of shirt manufacture, a huge industry employing mainly women was centred in Derry city. In the 1850s the sewing machine was introduced from America. The introduction of steam powered machines in the 1870s, gave a great boost to shirt factories. This was augmented by the addition of cutting machines which cut standard-sized pieces of fabric for making into shirts. By the early 1900s eighteen thousand people were employed in shirt factories, though there were many times that number of outworkers using sewing machines at home. Until 1925 this building was part of the Waterside Distillery complex. (D. Bigger and T. MacDonald)

LAPPING CLOTH FOR WRENS' UNIFORMS.
This photograph was taken on 29 February 1944 at William Clark & Sons, Upperlands, Co. Derry. In all, over 223 million yards were woven for war purposes in the factories of Northern Ireland. The original print of this photo bore the stamp 'passed by the censor for publication'. Clearly it was regarded as boosting production and morale. Coincidentally on the day this caption was being written, in 1993, the government announced the disbandment of the WRENS as a separate naval unit. (*Belfast Telegraph*)

PAINTING TABLECLOTHS, BALLYMENA, CO. ANTRIM, 26 JANUARY 1960.

Many damask tablecloths were enhanced by delicate painting. Skilled craftsmen and women made up a team under the supervision of highly trained designers, many of whom were graduates of the art department at Belfast College of Technology. (*Belfast Telegraph*)

GEORGE DUNCAN & SONS, MARKET SQUARE, LISBURN, CO. ANTRIM, *c.* 1910.
This draper's shop and textile store was established in 1836 and
retailed for nearly 100 years. It was next to the old market house
where brown or unbleached linen was sold 200 years ago. On this site
Lisburn Council has built the Irish Linen Centre, thus maintaining the
historic connection between the borough and the linen industry.
(Green Coll.)

ROBINSON & CLEAVER LTD, AND RICHARDSON SONS AND OWDEN'S LINEN WAREHOUSE, DONEGALL SQUARE, IN THE 1890s.
The Robinson & Cleaver's warehouse, on the left, was completed, to the design of Belfast architects Young and Mackenzie, in 1888. Mail order was of great importance to linen warehouses and the firm was so successful that in 1887 it was reckoned that between a third and a half of all parcels posted in Belfast were posted by Robinson & Cleaver. They employed thousands of outworkers throughout Ulster in producing their linen goods. The building on the right, designed by the eminent Belfast architects Lanyon, Lynn and Lanyon, as a warehouse for Richardson Sons & Owden's, is still one of Belfast's finest buildings. It now functions as part of Marks and Spencer's Belfast store. (Lawrence Coll.)

BARBOUR'S STAND AT THE WORLD'S FAIR, CHICAGO, 1893.

Linen manufacturers took part in international trade exhibitions all over the world. Attendance at these was indispensable in winning orders abroad. Irish linen was exhibited at all the great trade fairs that were a feature of nineteenth and early twentieth century international trade. These included The Great Exhibition at Crystal Palace in 1851, Vienna 1873, Paris 1889, Sydney 1879, Melbourne 1880, Buffalo 1901, Louisiana 1904, Brussels 1910, San Francisco 1910 and Wembley 1924–25. Thus the IDB trade missions abroad have a long pedigree. Prizes and medals from these exhibitions featured strongly in advertisements by many linen firms.
(Irish Linen Centre, Lisburn Museum)

THE WORLD'S FAIR AT CHICAGO, 1893.

Exhibit of Linen and Shoe Threads; Flax Embroidery and Lace Threads; Fishing Nets and Twines;

Shewn by

William Barbour & Sons, Ltd., Lisburn, Ireland

SPANISH LANGUAGE BILLBOARD (PROBABLY SPAIN) 9 JANUARY 1953.

As early as 1857, Spanish possessions, including the Canaries and islands in the Caribbean, were the second largest importers of Irish linen after the United States. Spain itself and Latin American countries made up nine of the top twenty export destinations.

The crumpled white linen suit became the hallmark of the gentleman in the tropics with cotton the preserve of the 'lower orders'. (*Belfast Telegraph*)

ADVERTISEMENT FOR OLD BLEACH, RANDALSTOWN, CO. ANTRIM, IN THE LATE 1930s.

Marketing was as important as production, and individual firms, the Irish Linen Guild and later the Northern Ireland government, devoted considerable resources to promotion and marketing. The promotion of linen concentrated on the luxury end of the market, extolling its virtues as a longlasting natural fibre and particularly the appeal of what a linen guild brochure described as its 'permanent beauty and gloss' in comparison with cotton and man-made fibres. (Hogg Coll.)

LORD BROOKEBOROUGH AT THE LINEN EXHIBITION, LONDON, 1962.
Lord Brookeborough, the Northern Ireland prime minister, is viewing a reproduction of the Bayeux tapestry. The original was also made of linen. The selling of Irish linen was a vitally important aspect of an industry whose motto could have been 'export to survive'. Larger manufacturers individually had sales and promotions departments with agencies all over the world but the Irish Linen Guild, set up in 1928 with offices in London, did this work on behalf of the industry as a whole and was supported by the Northern Ireland government because of its importance to the economy. (*Belfast Telegraph*)

THE LINEN INDUSTRY RESEARCH ASSOCIATION STAND AT THE LONDON LINEN EXHIBITION, 1962.

A sister organisation of the linen guild was the Lambeg Industrial Research Association set up in 1918. This provided solutions to manufacturing problems and the development of linen in combination with other fibres and the addition of new properties to better equip it for the marketplace. (*Belfast Telegraph*)

A BANQUETING CLOTH FOR THE AMERICAN CARDINAL SPELLMAN, IN THE 1950s.

The prestige of Irish linen earned it a place at the table of dignitaries the world over. This special cloth was woven at the handloom factory of John McCollum, Waringstown, by a veteran handloom weaver James Green, the order having been placed by a New York firm.

It was finished at Lambeg and later hand smoothed by Iris Carson, Lurgan. The tablecloth was of rose and trellis design and measured three and a half yards by eight yards. A special box was made for its transport to New York. (*Belfast Telegraph*)

WEAVERS' COTTAGES, MAIN STREET, WARINGSTOWN, CO. DOWN, *c.* 1915.
This was the first linen village. Houscs were built in the main street for weavers, in the early 18th century. The Rev. E.D. Atkinson, former rector of Waringstown, in his book *Recollections of an Ulster Archdeacon* (Belfast 1934) wrote: '*At that time (1900) almost every house had its weaving shop attached with two or three looms.*' (Green Coll.)

MOYALLON HOUSE, *c.* 1910.
Lying between Banbridge and Gilford, this was the family home of John Grubb Richardson, founder, with his brothers, of Bessbrook mill and model village. Members of the Richardson family can be seen on the steps. John G. Richardson died in 1891. Among his family papers is an offer from Gladstone in 1882 of a baronetcy for his lifetime of charitable work. This included caring for the linen workers of Bessbrook. He turned it down on the Quaker principle that virtue is its own reward. (Green Coll.)

SION HOUSE, SION MILLS, CO. TYRONE, IN THE EARLY 1900s.
The home of the Herdman family, this Elizabethan style mansion, with matching clock tower and gate lodge, was in the same architectural style, though in grander proportions, as the rest of the purpose-designed buildings of the village. (Cooper Coll.)

BESSBROOK MILLS, IN THE EARLY 1900s.

The linen trade had been carried on at Bessbrook as early as 1760 by the Pollock family. The property was bought in 1845 by the Quaker Richardsons, a family whose connection with linen went back to 1654. In 1878 the company became known as The Bessbrook Spinning Co. Ltd, though the Richardsons were still firmly in control. In 1913 the company operated 20,000 spindles and 760 looms making it the seventh largest Irish spinning and weaving firm. The Spinning Company closed down in 1973 throwing most employees out of work. The Ulster Weaving Company carried on the linen business at Bessbrook until 1987 when it moved all production to its Belfast headquarters. The Craigmore viaduct on the Great Northern Railway can be seen in the background. Railways were important in linking customers and suppliers. A railway siding ran right into the works. (Lawrence Coll.)

THE MILLS, SION MILLS IN THE 1900s.

The Herdman family built their mill in Sion Mills in the 1830s, the biblical allusion in the name reflecting the religious attitude of the family. The site was chosen in an area where water power was plentiful, the strength of the mill-race being clearly illustrated here. The village was a model in layout and the design of the buildings. In the 1913 survey of the Irish linen industry in the directory of John Warrall (Ltd) of Oldham, Herdman's was the fifth biggest spinning firm with 26,000 spindles. Mill girls in wet spinning areas wore a 'glazer', an oil cloth or rubber apron, usually yellow in colour. This gave rise to the nickname 'yellowbelly' and to a street-game song:

> *Sion Mills is a nice wee place*
> *It's surrounded by a hill*
> *And if you want a yellow girl*
> *You'll get her in the mill.* (Welch Coll.)

TERRACE OF LINEN WORKERS' HOUSES, SION MILLS, CO. TYRONE.

This picture, taken in the 1900s, shows hens in front of the houses. It was a feature of villages like this that domestic animals such as hens, pigs and goats were kept to supplement the diet and income of mill and factory workers. This was even the case with linen workers in Belfast. In fact the effluent from the many pigs kept in the backyards of the Falls and Shankill was cited as a major health hazard in the Belfast Corporation Inquiry into the death rate in 1896. (Cooper Coll.)

CHARLEMONT SQUARE, BESSBROOK, CO. ARMAGH, *c.* 1900.
Completed in 1855 it was, like much of the original village, built from granite blocks quarried locally on the estate of Viscount Charlemont, former owner of the land on which Bessbrook was built and from whom the square gets its name. This quarry supplied granite for the building of Manchester Town Hall, and the great steps of St George's Hall, Liverpool. A green in the middle of the square was later converted into a play area for children. (Lawrence Coll.)

THE BESSBROOK TRAM, 6 JULY 1945.

This began running on 1 October 1885 to link the village with Newry. It used electricity generated at nearby Millvale. The track was exactly three miles long. It was only the second electric tramway in Britain, the one at Giant's Causeway being a few months older. As well as workers and passengers it carried coal and raw materials to the mill and finished products in the opposite direction to the docks or railway station in Newry. It closed on 10 January 1948 having become unviable due to declining mill traffic and competition from road haulage. (*Belfast Telegraph*)

SION SPORTS, SION MILLS, CO. TYRONE, 1909.
The annual sports day was an important event in the fostering of a community spirit in the village, encouraged by the Herdman family. It is recorded here in postcard form by the Strabane based photographer Cooper. Sion Mills, like many linen areas, has a long cricketing tradition. Indeed it was on the Sion Mills ground that Ireland recorded their historic victory over the West Indies in 1969. (Cooper Coll.)

WORKERS' READING ROOM AND DINING HALL, DRUMANESS, CO. DOWN, IN THE 1960s.
This building was erected by the mill owners, Charles James Hurst to supplement existing facilities. It has an ornamental clock tower, a glazed tile entrance porch and a large dining hall on the ground floor. On the first floor was a reading room, with pitch pine panelling, and a snooker room. Outside, the tower and upper gable walls were decorated with timber cladding and plaster. Healthy recreation, such as cricket and soccer, was encouraged by the owners and Miss Pleasant Hurst, a member of the family in the late Victorian period, organised religious plays for the workers. No licensed premises were allowed in the mill village. (McCutcheon Coll.)

HILLSIDE, DRUMANESS, CO. DOWN, IN THE 1960s.
These fine dwellings, consisting of two terraces of a total of fifteen houses, were built by the company in 1906. At this time there were about 300 workers living in the village and the surrounding townlands. In 1909/10 the estimated value of the housing stock in Drumaness was £6,910, giving an estimated return on gross rents of 8.9%. In the 1900s the average weekly rent of a kitchen house was 3 shillings, at a time when a skilled worker in linen earned around 28 shillings a week. As in all mill villages, repairs were done by tradesmen employed by the company, which kept costs down. (McCutcheon Coll.)

QUALITY ROW, MAIN STREET, DONAGHCLONEY, CO. DOWN, IN THE 1960s.

This terrace of parlour houses completed in 1891, was appropriately named, being of a high specification. Donaghcloney, largely rebuilt by William Liddell in the 1890s and early 1900s, using John Graham Builders, of nearby Dromore, was typical of mill villages in that the company provided housing, education and recreation for the workers.

Amateur drama was greatly encouraged by the Liddells. The village grew from a population of 148 and 30 houses in 1861 to 399 inhabitants in 83 houses in 1911. Of the 1000 employees in 1911, only 150 lived in the village. The William Liddell Memorial school erected by his sons in 1904 is now a church. (McCutcheon Coll.)

THE CRICKET PAVILION, DONAGHCLONEY, CO. DOWN, IN THE 1960s.

William Liddell's four sons were educated at Christ's College, Finchley, where they gained a love of cricket. They became members of the North of Ireland club in Belfast. They introduced the game to their workers in Donaghcloney, where the first ground was at Banoge House, the Liddell home. The present ground was built next to the factory, with a cycle track around the perimeter. The pavilion in this photograph was built in 1901 at a cost of £131 paid by the family. It is 33 feet by 20 feet. The club was supported financially by the Liddell family, local tradesmen and weekly deductions from the wages of worker members. (McCutcheon Coll.)

WORKERS' COTTAGES, DRUMNAGALLY, BANBRIDGE, CO. DOWN IN THE 1960s.

Of course not all workers in the rural linen industry were fortunate in their living conditions. These cottages, built by F.W. Hayes, are in Drumnagally in the parish of Seapatrick. Often employers would construct rows of houses to a very much lower specification for low-skilled workers. The houses in this picture contrast poorly with those seen in the earlier mill village pictures. They are unusual in being built in brick at the front and stone at the back. (McCutcheon Coll.)

THE WHITE LINEN HALL, BELFAST, *c.* 1870.

Occupying the centre of Donegall Square from 1785 until its demolition in 1896 to make way for the new city hall, it was a symbol of the growing linen trade in Belfast. However, by the end of its existence, it had long ceased to fulfil its original function of linen market and exchange. Many of the other industries in the city, such as engineering grew in association with the needs of the linen industry. Belfast's rapid expansion as a city coincided with that of linen which helped to give it prestige. Equally the decline in linen after the first world war brought in its train a decline in the prosperity of the city. (Lawrence Coll.)

WAREHOUSES AND OFFICES, BEDFORD STREET, *c.*1900.
Bedford Street with its stately offices and warehouses could at one time have been called the headquarters of the linen industry. Most buying and selling of the finished linen product occurred in and around Bedford Street. The Ulster Hall has strong connections with the linen industry, in that the giant Mulholland organ costing £3,000 was donated by Andrew Mulholland, of the York Street Mill. Many of these buildings have fallen on hard times but a series of murals, depicting the history of the industry, was placed in boarded up windows of one building in September 1994, on the initiative of Peter McLachlan of the charity Bryson House. (Lawrence Coll.)

STAIRCASE AT ROBINSON CLEAVER, DONEGALL
SQUARE, *c.* 1890.

While the upper floors of the building held packing and
dispatch departments, the ground floor housed a grand
linen emporium. When this bulding was converted to shops
and office units, in the 1980s, the staircase was removed to
Ballyedmond, Rostrevor, Co. Down. (Lawrence Coll.)

YORK STREET MILL, OF THE YORK STREET FLAX SPINNING AND WEAVING CO. LTD, TAKEN IN THE 1930s.
Founded in 1830 by Alexander Mulholland, it was the first of its kind in Ireland. The company had both the biggest spinning mill and weaving factory in the world. It employed over 4,000 people not counting outworkers. The company had branches and agencies all over the world, like most of the other major linen firms. It was a Belfast landmark until the Second World War. (*Belfast Telegraph*)

YORK STREET MILL AFTER THE BLITZ OF 4/5 MAY 1941.
The destruction of York Street mill by incendiaries was the largest fire ever seen in the city. The six storey building stood on a site 100 yards by 300 yards. No one was killed but it was a serious blow to the economy and morale of the city. As late as 8 March 1943, this photograph bore the stamp of the military security office, '*no objection to prints of this photograph being made provided they are not published in any manner*'. In many ways the destruction of York Street Mill was symbolic of the end of an era for an industry and a city that had already passed their zenith. (*Belfast Telegraph*)

JENNYMOUNT MILL AND HOUSES, NORTH
DERBY STREET, NORTH BELFAST, *c.* 1905.
These houses were built by Philip Johnston & Co.,
Flaxspinners, for spinning masters and labourers, an
unusual juxtaposition of ranks in the same housing, in
that the master was a supervisor while the labourer was
at the bottom of the ladder in the mill. (Hogg Coll.)

TERRACE HOUSES, SCOTCH STREET, LOWER FALLS, BELFAST, IN THE 1960s.
This was taken prior to demolition and redevelopment. For many linen workers in Belfast, particularly those in the less-skilled occupations, living conditions were very bad compounding the misery of their poor working conditions. Overcrowding and poor sanitation led to frequent epidemics of diseases like typhoid. Many houses had an outside toilet leading to the colloquial euphemism 'going to the yard'. The worst-off shared an outside communal privy and a cold watertap. (Belfast Exposed)

BARBOUR RESIDENCE, FINAGHY, NEAR BELFAST, 1924.
The great houses on the shores of Belfast Lough and in south Belfast arose mostly from fortunes made in linen. This house had its own schoolroom for the family children, appropriately as it now belongs to Hunterhouse College. The main residence of the Barbour family was Clanwilliam House, now known as Danesfort, the present headquarters of Northern Ireland Electricity. (Welch Coll.)

LIGONIEL HOUSE, BELFAST 1930.
This fine dwelling was provided by Ewarts for the manager of
their Mountain Mill. Mr. Gull the manager can be seen in the
doorway. (Hogg Coll.)

LOOPBRIDGE WEAVING FACTORY, LISMORE STREET, BELFAST, 12 MAY 1937.
These women are celebrating the coronation of George VI in the traditional way with machinery bedecked with bunting. In the early days of the century trade unions had a struggle to get some, otherwise loyal, linen employers to grant a holiday to their workers on such royal occasions. (Hogg Coll.)

CHILDREN OF MARY, CORPUS CHRISTI PROCESSION, FALLS ROAD, BELFAST IN THE 1950s.

Most of the women in this religious procession were linen workers. Membership of Catholic sodalities like the Children of Mary was especially high among the girls of the mills and factories of the Falls Road. The streets through which this procession wended its way were built by the linen firms to house their employees. Some, such as Malcolmson Street, bore the family name of the owner. (Belfast Exposed)

ARCH IN DONEGALL SQUARE ERECTED FOR THE ROYAL VISIT IN 1885.
Note the symbolic references to the importance of linen with the spinning wheel on top and the bales of linen within the arch. Three years later Queen Victoria conferred the title and status of city on Belfast. This was in recognition of its enormous growth, in only a few decades, which would not have been possible without the linen industry. (Lawrence Coll.)

SPORTING DAYS AT MOSSLEY, CO. ANTRIM, *c.* 1923.
This photograph was taken at the opening of the Mossley sports pavilion. John Patterson came to Mossley mill as manager in 1920 and started a guild to look after the general recreation of the workers. This included weekly cinema shows, concerts, a bowling green, two hockey pitches, tennis courts and a children's playground. (Mrs S. Seaton)

OUTING ON A WORK'S LORRY, BALLYCLARE, CO. ANTRIM, *c.* 1920.

A Kirkpatrick's of Ballyclare lorry outing with chairs on the back perched rather precariously. For many linen workers a holiday for more than a few days was out of the question and day excursions were very important until after the Second World War. These were provided by employers for whole departments or by trade unions and even by the Nationalist MP for West Belfast, Joe Devlin, in 'Wee Joe's Excursions' for workers from the Falls and Shankill Roads. Portrush was the main destination. The provision in the post-war period of recreation clubs and sports centres such as Ewart's Recreation showed the appreciation by more enlightened employers of the importance of a happier healthier workforce. (L. Gordon)

POWERLOOM TENTERS AND OVERLOOKERS OUTING, GREYABBEY, CO. DOWN, 1923.
This is a picture from the collection of William Topping. He was a damask weaver and active trade unionist, being at one time a committee member of the Powerloom Tenters' Union of Ireland and secretary of the Foreman Loom Overlookers' Association. Tenters were overseers in charge of a number of looms. Topping is not in the picture as, being a keen amateur photographer, he probably took it himself. His excursions used two buses curiously nicknamed 'big nut' and 'little nut'. (PRONI)

CRICKET AT 'THE LAWN', WARINGSTOWN, CO. DOWN, 1 JUNE 1956.
In common with other linen areas such as Lisburn, Donaghcloney and
Sion Mills, Waringstown was and still is a great centre for cricket.

Workers were often encouraged in the pastime by their employers.
(*Belfast Telegraph*)

MISS BELFAST, 1927.
Linen Industry parade outside Belfast College of Technology, featuring Miss Belfast 1927. This reflects also the close relation between the college and the industry and its important input into textile design. (Hogg Coll.)

FITTERS, BLACKSTAFF SPINNING AND WEAVING CO. LTD, SPRINGFIELD ROAD, WEST BELFAST, IN THE 1950s.
Back row 2nd left Billy Donaghy, Lisburn, fitter (mill end), 2nd right back row John Scott, spinning room fitter. Front row with cat, Jack Palmer, Glenwood Street, Shankill Road, labourer. Behind him sitting, Jack Skates, fitter, Low Road, Lisburn, came from Rose Cottage, Purdysburn. John Scott later worked in mill fitting at Ewart's Belfast and Campbell Barbour at Mossley, Co. Antrim. These men were close friends in and out of work but they had to be ready for a ribbing. They tied one worker's bicycle to the rafters of the mechanic shop and he had to walk home. If a workmate was getting married, they oiled him from head to toe. (Mrs M. Scott)

BLACKSTAFF WEFT WINDERS' OUTING, BALLYCARRY, CO. ANTRIM, 1951.

In the picture are, left, Margaret Irvine, right, Margaret Scott, then living in Canmore Street, Shankill Road, Belfast and her sister Jeannie. Margaret Scott was taught weft winding at the Blackstaff by her sister Martha Mahood. She started work in July and worked from 8am to 6pm. They worked in a winding room which never heated up in winter, standing on tiled floors, their feet like ice. In summer it got so hot that they whitewashed the windows. They only had two days off at Easter, Christmas and July. Saturday work had only just been done away with. In what leisure time they had they went dancing, to the pictures and keep fit. (Mrs M. Scott)

BIBLIOGRAPHY

Betty Messenger, *Picking up the linen threads* (Belfast, 1988).

W.H. Crawford, *The Irish linen industry* (Ulster Folk and Transport Museum, 1987).

Linen, continuity and change, The story of the Irish linen industry (Ulster Folk and Transport Museum, 1987).

P. Ollerenshaw, 'Industry 1820–1914' in L. Kennedy and P. Ollerenshaw eds. *An economic history of Ulster* (Manchester, 1985).

E. Boyle, 'Linenopolis: the rise of the textile industry' in J.C. Beckett et al. *Belfast, the making of the city 1800–1914* (Belfast, 1983).

A life in Linenopolis, the memoirs of William Topping, Belfast damask weaver, 1903–56, edited with an introduction by E. O'Connor and T. Parkhill (Belfast, 1992).

P. McDonnell, *They wrought among the tow; flax and linen in County Tyrone 1750–1900* (Belfast, 1990).

W.A. McCutcheon, *The industrial archaeology of Northern Ireland* (Belfast, 1980).

E.R.R. Green, *The Lagan valley 1800–1850* (London, 1949).

W.H. Crawford, *Domestic industry in Ireland: The experience of the linen industry* (Dublin, 1972).

W.H. Crawford, *The handloom weavers and the Ulster linen industry* (Belfast, 1994).

Industries of the north, one hundred years ago (Belfast, 1986).

G.H. Bassett, *County Down 100 years ago, a guide and directory, 1886* (Belfast, 1988).

G.H. Bassett, *County Armagh 100 years ago, a guide and directory, 1888* (Belfast, 1989).

ACKNOWLEDGEMENTS

The photographs in this book are from different sources in both private and public hands. I would like to thank the following for permission to publish material from their various collections; the trustees of the Ulster Museum, the Hogg and Welch Collections; the trustees of the Ulster Folk and Transport Museum, the Green Collection; Lisburn Museum; the Deputy Keeper, the Public Record Office of Northern Ireland (PRONI), the Cooper Collection and other photographs including those on pages 44 and 45 for which additional acknowledgement is due to Messrs H. and B. J. Bell and page 85 for which thanks is due to Peter Topping; the National Library of Ireland, the Lawrence Collection; HMSO Department of the Environment (Northern Ireland), Monuments and Buildings Record, the McCutcheon Collection; Belfast Exposed and the *Belfast Telegraph* photograph library. I would like to thank the staff of all these institutions and in particular Dr Vivienne Pollock and Pauline Dixon of the Ulster Museum, Trevor Parkhill of PRONI, Terence Reeves-Smyth of the DOE, Brian Mackey Curator, and Elaine Flanigan of Lisburn Museum, Sally Skilling of UFTM, and Peter Bainbridge, photographic manager and Peter King of the *Belfast Telegraph*. I wish also to thank Kevin Rosato, Falls Community Council, Sean McKernan of Belfast Exposed, Seamus Sammon and Jim McKee of the Dunlewey Centre and Desmond FitzGerald of Armagh. I am grateful to Jack McKinney, the Ballyclare and District Historical Society and Mrs Sadie Seaton for permission to use the photographs on pages 37, 38, 42, 83 and 84. Also from private sources came photographs belonging to Mrs Margaret Scott, a former linen worker and Maynard Sinton of the family firm of Thomas Sinton in Tandragee. Dr Bill Crawford of the Federation for Ulster Local Studies gave valuable advice on the domestic linen industry as did Dr Denis MacNeice on mill villages. At Friar's Bush Press, I would like to thank Dr Brian Walker who originally commissioned this work and continued to provide encouragement, Jane Crosbie for her help and especially Margaret McNulty for all her advice.